Copyright © 2012 Brenda Neugent
All rights reserved.
ISBN: 1470158469
ISBN-13: 987-1470158460

DEDICATION

This book is dedicated to my husband, who helped test each
and every one of these recipes. I love you!!!

There's an old joke in the Midwest told around harvest season: Don't leave your car unlocked, because your neighbor is likely to use the opportunity to fill it with all his unwanted zucchini.

But the delicate flavor of the summer squash with skin that ranges from light green to almost black makes it one of the most versatile of the summer vegetables, able to star in both sweet and savory dishes.

Plus, it offers Vitamin C, folate, potassium (more than in a banana), beta carotene and Vitamin A, along with a low calorie count because of its high water content.

The zucchini is easy to grow, and a single plant can yield up to 10 pounds of squash. Because it is so prolific, it has long been one of my favorites, and I have been experimenting in my kitchen for years to come up with new ways to take advantage of the delicious zucchini.

I hope that after trying a few, you'll be thrilled when your neighbor leaves any excess produce on your back porch, and find yourself begging for more.

Recipes

Sauces & Condiments

- Zucchini Pickles, 10
- Sweet Zucchini Relish, 10
- Fresh Veggie Salsa, 11
- Greek Yogurt Sauce, 11
- Fruity Zucchini Salsa, 12
- Pickled Zucchini Slices, 12
- Zucchini & Apple Butter, 13

Appetizers

- Zucchini Chips, 16
- Zucchini Meatballs in Garlic Cream Sauce, 16
- Zucchini Rumaki, 17
- Zucchini Fries, 17
- Mini Italian Sliders with Spicy Mustard Sauce, 18
- Stuffed Mushrooms with Cheese Sauce, 19
- Mozzarella Zucchini Sticks, 20
- Zucchini and Corn Fritters with Zucchini and Apple Dipping Sauce, 21
- Mexican Dip, 22
- Zucchini Bean Dip, 23
- Zucchini Tarts, 24
- Miniature Zucchini Wellingtons, 25

Soups

- Creamy Zucchini Soup, 28
- Roasted Vegetable Soup, 28
- California Vegetable Cheese Soup, 29
- Veggie and Chicken Soup, 30
- Mexican Tortilla Soup, 31

Breads & Muffins

- Sweet Spiced Zucchini Bread, 34
- Lemon Zucchini Bread, 35
- Chocolate Zucchini Sweet Bread, 36
- Spiced Blueberry Pie Muffins, 37
- Glazed Lemon Poppy Seed Muffins, 38
- Chocolate Chip Muffins, 39
- Oatmeal Zucchini Muffins, 40
- Spicy Zucchini Cornbread, 41
- Savory Zucchini Multigrain Bread, 42

Sandwiches

- Mega Pizza Roll, 44
- Grilled Zucchini and Caramelized Onion Sandwich, 45
- Sloppy Joes, 46
- Zucchini Meatball Sub, 47
- Italian Marinated Vegetable Sandwich, 48

Breakfast

- Zucchini Buttermilk Pancakes, 50
- Italian Zucchini Strata, 51
- Zucchini and Spinach Frittata, 52
- Breakfast Skillet, 53
- Tomato and Zucchini Pie, 54

Salads

- Zucchini Pasta Salad, 56
- Zucchini Citrus Salad, 56
- Grilled Zucchini and Steak Salad, 57
- Caprese Salad with Grilled Zucchini, 58
- Spring Zucchini Orzo Salad, 59
- Creamy Vegetable Coleslaw, 59
- Marinated Vegetable Salad, 60

Side dishes

- Stuffed Zucchini, 62
- Parmesan Baked Zucchini, 63
- Grilled Zucchini, 63
- Layered Zucchini & Tomatoes, 64
- Potato-Zucchini Hash Browns, 65
- Zucchini & Cheese Soufflé, 66
- Sautéed Zucchini in Cheese Sauce, 67
- Zucchini and Spinach Sauté, 67
- Ratatouille, 68
- Zucchini Lasagna, 69
- Creamy Spiced Zucchini, 70
- Italian Zucchini, 70
- Zucchini in Brown Butter and Sage Sauce, 71
- Zucchini and Cauliflower Mash, 71
- Scalloped Zucchini and Potatoes, 72

Main dishes

- Japanese Steakhouse Venison, 74
- One-Pot Zucchini Casserole, 75
- Zucchini & Mushroom Meatloaf, 76
- Veggie Stuffed Meatloaf, 77
- Loaded Chicken Parmesan, 78
- Zucchini Parmesan, 79
- Zucchini Risotto, 80
- Loaded Venison Spaghetti, 81
- Creamy Italian Pasta, 82
- Won't-Miss-the-Meat Vegetable Lasagna, 83
- Chicken and Zucchini Linguini, 84
- Zucchini-Spinach Quiche, 85
- Shrimp Fettuccini, 86
- Veggie-Stuffed Macaroni & Cheese, 87
- Cheesy Beef and Macaroni Casserole, 88
- Bacon-Infused Chicken and Zucchini over Jasmine Rice, 89
- Zucchini and Sausage with Polenta Cakes, 90
- Fire Roasted Vegetable Pasta, 91
- Zucchini & Mushroom Tart, 92
- Stuffed Zucchini Rolls, 93
- Manicotti with Zucchini & Italian Sausage Filling, 94
- Curried Chicken & Veggies, 95
- Zucchini, Basil and Bacon Pizza, 96

Desserts

- **Zucchini Citrus Cake**, 98
- **Banana Pudding Cake**, 99
- **Chocolate Zucchini Sheet Cake**, 100
- **Zucchini-Pineapple Pound Cake**, 101
- **Zucchini Spice Cake**, 102
- **Walnut and Sour Cream Pound Cake**, 103
- **Clementine and Zucchini Cake**, 104
- **Triple Chocolate Zucchini Brownies**, 105
- **Zucchini Cookies**, 106
- **Zucchini Cowboy Cookies**, 107
- **Zucchini Date Bars**, 108
- **Rustic Zucchini Tart**, 109
- **Zucchini-Watermelon Sorbet**, 110

SAUCES
&
CONDIMENTS

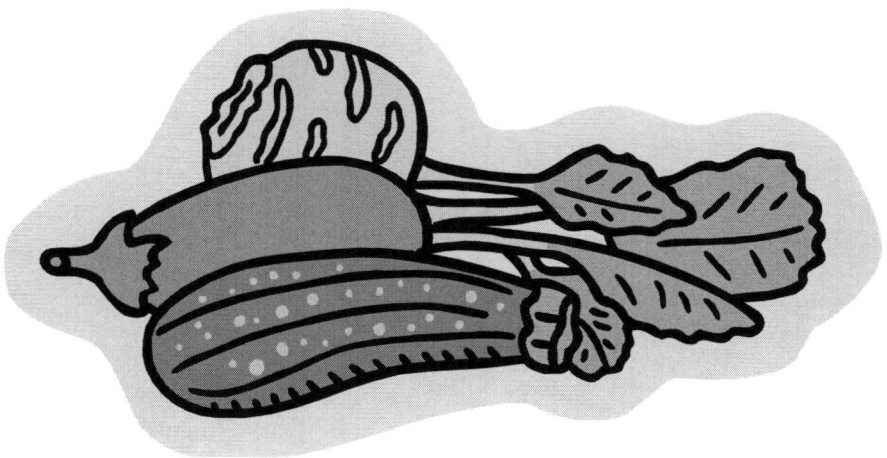

Whether sweet or savory, the versatile zucchini is a great choice for zesty relishes, crunchy salsa and sweet, buttery spreads.

Zucchini Pickles

- **1 zucchini, thinly sliced**
- **1 cup champagne vinegar**
- **½ cup white sugar**
- **2 teaspoons pickling spices**
- **1 clove garlic, smashed**
- **1 star anise**
- **2 allspice berries**

1. Mix together champagne vinegar, sugar, pickling spices, garlic, star anise and allspice berries in a small saucepan. Bring mixture to a boil.
2. Place zucchini slices in a small casserole or large bowl and pour liquid over the slices so they're completely submerged.
3. Cover the top of the casserole or bowl with plastic wrap and allow the mixture to cool completely.
4. Drain and serve.

This recipe is especially nice with pulled pork sandwiches.

Sweet Zucchini Relish

- **1 zucchini, finely diced**
- **1 onion, finely diced**
- **½ green bell pepper, finely diced**
- **½ cup apple cider vinegar**
- **½ cup water**
- **½ cup brown sugar**
- **¼ teaspoon salt**
- **Pinch mustard seeds**

1. Mix ingredients in a medium saucepan and bring to a boil.
2. Cook until mixture is thick and most of the liquid has turned to syrup.
3. Chill and serve with burgers, hot dogs or brats.

Fresh Veggie Salsa

- 1 medium tomato, finely diced
- 1 medium zucchini, finely diced
- ½ red bell pepper, finely diced
- ½ purple onion, finely diced
- 1 small hot pepper, finely diced
- ¼ cup cilantro leaves
- 1 tablespoon olive oil
- ¼ teaspoon salt

1. Mix vegetables in a medium-sized bowl and add cilantro, olive oil and salt.
2. Allow flavors to meld for at least 30 minutes before serving.
3. Serve with tortilla chips.

Greek Yogurt Sauce

- 1 zucchini, peeled and chopped
- 1 cup Greek yogurt
- 1 clove garlic
- 1 tablespoon loosely packed cilantro leaves, snipped
- Salt and pepper to taste

1. Mix ingredients and blend in a food processor until blended.
2. Chill and serve with falafel or as a sauce for gyros.

Fruity Zucchini Salsa

- **2 zucchini, diced**
- **1 mango, diced**
- **1 can pineapple tidbits with juice**
- **Dash red pepper flakes**
1. Mix zucchini, mango and pineapple with juice.
2. Add red pepper flakes and chill well.
3. Serve with salmon, turkey burgers or as a fruity topping for chicken salad sandwiches.

Pickled Zucchini Slices

- **2 zucchini**
- **1 cup champagne vinegar**
- **½ cup sugar**
- **¼ cup water**
- **1 cinnamon stick**
- **1 star anise**
- **1 teaspoon whole allspice**
- **1 teaspoon whole cloves**
- **Pinch black peppercorns**
- **Pinch salt**
1. Cut zucchini into four lengthwise slices, removing seeded core but retaining the skin. Cut those slices into one-inch pieces.
2. Bring vinegar, sugar, water, cinnamon stick, star anise, allspice, cloves, peppercorns and salt to a boil in a medium saucepan.
3. Add zucchini slices and boil for about 5 minutes.
4. Remove from heat and chill zucchini slices in the pickling liquid.
5. Serve this sweet treat as an appetizer, a tasty garnish on a plate or a sweet snack.

Zucchini and Apple Butter

- **2 zucchini, peeled and chopped**
- **1 small apple, cored, peeled and chopped**
- **½ cup sugar**
- **¼ cup water**
- **1 teaspoon cinnamon**
- **1/8 teaspoon ground allspice**
- **1/8 teaspoon cloves**

1. Mix ingredients in a large saucepan and cook over low heat until mixture is thick and begins to caramelize, about two hours.
2. Mix in a food processor until smooth and creamy.
3. This sweet treat is perfect on toast, scones or biscuits.

APPETIZERS

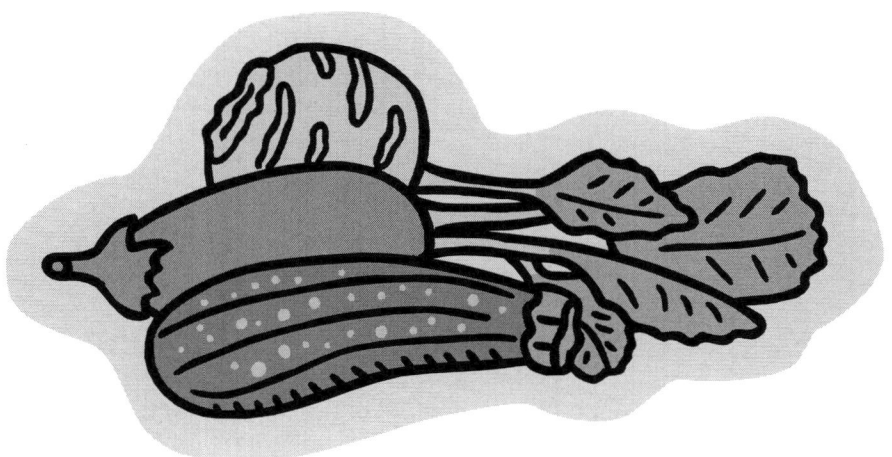

This tasty collection – from amuse-bouche bites to tasty sliders – can turn any party into a flavorful opportunity to showcase the zucchini.

Zucchini Chips

- Three medium-sized zucchini
- Two tablespoons olive oil
- 1/4 cup Italian-seasoned bread crumbs
- 1/4 cup Parmesan cheese
- Salt and pepper to taste
1. Preheat oven to 450 degrees.
2. Slice zucchini in quarter-inch rounds and pat dry. Drizzle olive oil over the zucchini slices in a bowl and toss until well coated.
3. Blend bread crumbs and cheese in a separate bowl and dip each slice of zucchini in the mixture, coating evenly.
4. Place slices on a non-stick baking sheet and bake for 25 to 30 minutes, until coating is browned and crunchy.

Zucchini Meatballs in Garlic Cream Sauce

- 1 pound ground meat, a blend of beef, pork and Italian sausage
- 1 medium zucchini, shredded
- ½ cup bread crumbs
- 1 egg
- 1 teaspoon salt
- ½ teaspoon pepper
1. Blend mixture well with hands and shape into balls.
2. Fry in vegetable oil seasoned with crushed red pepper until well browned.
3. Serve in Garlic Cream Sauce.

Garlic Cream Sauce: Sauté three cloves minced garlic in two tablespoons melted butter until it becomes aromatic, about one or two minutes. Add one cup milk, half cup heavy whipping cream, two tablespoons flour and salt and pepper to taste. Wisk until well blended and cook on low heat until sauce thickens, stirring constantly. Pour over meatballs.

Zucchini Rumaki

- 1 medium-sized zucchini
- 8 slices bacon, sliced in half
- 2 tablespoons brown sugar
- 2 tablespoons soy sauce
- 2 tablespoons olive oil
- 2 tablespoons balsamic vinegar
- ¼ teaspoon garlic powder

1. Slice zucchini into four chunks, then quarter each piece.
2. Mix brown sugar, soy sauce, oil, balsamic vinegar and garlic powder.
3. Add zucchini, marinating for several hours.
4. Remove zucchini and discard marinade.
5. Wrap each piece of zucchini in a slice of bacon, securing with a toothpick.
6. Broil for 10 to 12 minutes, turning halfway, until bacon is crispy.

Zucchini Fries

- 2 medium zucchini, julienned, with seeds discarded
- Peanut oil
- Sea salt

1. After slicing, place zucchini on paper towels to absorb moisture.
2. Working in handfuls, drop zucchini into hot peanut oil, cooking until shreds are browned and crispy.
3. Dry on paper towels to absorb excess oil and sprinkle with sea salt. Serve hot.

Mini Italian Sliders

- **8 ounces Italian sausage**
- **1 medium zucchini, shredded**
- **½ cup bread crumbs**
- **½ cup flour**
- **1 egg**
- **1 teaspoon salt**
- **½ teaspoon black pepper**
- **One tablespoons olive oil**
1. Combine ingredients and mix well.
2. Shape into patties and fry in hot vegetable oil until sausage is no longer pink and outside of patties are brown and crispy, about 10 to 15 minutes.
3. Serve with Spicy Mustard Sauce

Spicy Mustard Sauce: Blend ½ cup sour cream, 2 tablespoons spicy mustard, 1 tablespoon heavy cream, black pepper to taste and a dash of smoked paprika.

Stuffed Mushrooms with Cheese Sauce

- 16 ounces white mushrooms, stems removed and reserved
- ½ cup onion
- 3 cloves garlic, minced
- 4 ounces lean ground beef
- ½ cup shredded zucchini
- ½ cup chopped mushroom stems
- ½ cup bread crumbs
- ½ cup shredded sharp cheddar cheese
- Cheese Sauce (Recipe below)

1. Preheat oven to 375 degrees.
2. Sauté onion and garlic in olive oil until onion is tender.
3. Add ground beef and cook until meat is no longer pink, crumbling it as it browns.
4. Add shredded zucchini and mushroom stems and cook until veggies are soft and tender.
5. Add bread crumbs and shredded cheese; mix well.
6. Stuff mixture into mushroom caps and arrange mushrooms in a 9x13-inch baking pan.
7. Pour cheese sauce over mushrooms and bake for about 30 minutes.

Cheese Sauce: Melt two tablespoons of butter over medium heat. Add two tablespoons of flour and mix until smooth. Add 1 ½ cups milk and cook until thickened and bubbly. Add 4 ounces Velveeta cheese and 1 cup shredded sharp cheddar cheese. Stir until melted.

Mozzarella Zucchini Sticks

- 1 8-ounce package sliced mozzarella cheese
- 1 medium zucchini, cut into thin slices
- 1 cup flour
- 1 egg, beaten
- 1 cup unseasoned bread crumbs
- 1 cup all-purpose flour
- ½ teaspoon garlic powder
- ½ teaspoon onion powder
- ¼ teaspoon black pepper
- Marinara sauce, optional.

1. Allow sliced mozzarella to come to room temperature.
2. Slice zucchini into slivers that are the same length as the cheese slices.
3. Beat egg until frothy.
4. Mix bread crumbs, flour and spices.
5. Roll cheese around zucchini slivers and dip into flour.
6. Dip sticks into egg mixture and drop into bread crumb mixture.
7. Fry in hot oil until breading is brown and crispy.
8. Serve with marinara sauce, if desired.

Zucchini and Corn Fritters with Zucchini & Apple Dipping Sauce

- One cup flour
- One cup cornmeal
- ¼ cup sugar
- 1 tablespoon baking powder
- 1 teaspoon salt
- 1 medium zucchini, shredded
- 1 cup whole kernel corn; fresh, frozen or canned
- 2 eggs
- 1 cup milk
- 4 tablespoons melted butter
- Peanut oil for frying

1. Whisk together dry ingredients and set aside.
2. Beat eggs and add the milk, blending until well mixed.
3. Add egg mixture to dry ingredients and mix just until blended.
4. Fold in zucchini, corn and melted butter.
5. Drop by spoonful until hot oil, turning the fritter when the bottom side is well browned and crispy.
6. Dry on paper towels and serve with Zucchini and Apple Dipping Sauce.

ZUCCHINI AND APPLE DIPPING SAUCE: Melt 1 tablespoon of butter in a saucepan and add ½ cup brown sugar, ½ cup water, 1 teaspoon apple cider vinegar, one finely diced peeled apple and one finely diced peeled zucchini. Bring the mixture to a boil and cook until the zucchini and apple are tender and the sauce is thick and bubbly.

Mexican Dip

- **1 pound ground beef**
- **1 cup chopped onion**
- **1 cup chopped green bell pepper**
- **2 cups shredded zucchini**
- **1 heaping teaspoon ground cumin**
- **8 ounces shredded sharp Cheddar cheese**
- **8 ounces Velveeta cheese**
- **1 14-ounce can tomatoes with chilies**
- **1 cup salsa**
- **2 cups shredded lettuce**
- **1 cup sour cream**
- **1 small can sliced black olives**
- **1 tomato, chopped**

1. Coat a sauté pan with olive oil and add onion, bell pepper and ground cumin, sautéing until onions are translucent and peppers are beginning to become tender.
2. Add beef and cook until meat is browned,
3. Add zucchini and sauté for about five minutes, allowing moisture to be released and cooked off.
4. Add Velveeta cheese and canned tomatoes, stirring until cheese is melted.
5. Spread onto a platter.
6. Top with lettuce, fresh tomato, black olives and Cheddar cheese, followed by dollops of sour cream and salsa.
7. Serve with tortilla chips.

Zucchini Bean Dip

- 1 medium zucchini, chopped
- 1 cup chopped mushrooms
- 2 tablespoons olive oil
- 2 cloves garlic, minced
- ½ tablespoon Italian seasoning
- ½ teaspoon crushed red pepper
- ¼ teaspoon onion powder
- 1 cup white beans
- ½ cup sour cream

1. Preheat oven to 400 degrees.
2. Place zucchini and mushrooms in a bowl.
3. Drizzle with olive oil, garlic, Italian seasoning, crushed red pepper and onion powder.
4. Toss zucchini and mushrooms until well coated.
5. Roast in a 400 degree oven until tender and caramelized.
6. Blend zucchini and mushrooms in a food processor until smooth. Add white beans and 2 tablespoons water and mix until smooth.
7. Spoon mixture into a bowl and add sour cream, salt and pepper to taste and mix well.
8. Serve chilled with crackers or garlic toasts.

Zucchini Tarts

- 16 sheets phyllo dough, thawed
- 1 tablespoon melted butter
- 1 tablespoon olive oil
- ½ yellow onion, finely diced
- ½ red bell pepper, finely diced
- 1 cup ground turkey
- 2 garlic cloves, minced
- Dash red pepper flakes
- ¼ teaspoon fennel seeds
- ¼ teaspoon Italian seasoning
- 1 medium zucchini, finely shredded
- ¼ cup heavy cream
- ½ cup shredded mozzarella cheese
- ¼ cup shredded cheddar cheese
- ¼ cup shredded Parmesan cheese

1. Preheat oven to 350 degrees.
2. Spray eight cupcake-sized tart cups with non-stick cooking spray.
3. Heat olive oil in a sauté pan and add onions and bell pepper, cooking until both a slightly soft.
4. Add ground turkey, garlic, red pepper flakes, Italian seasoning and fennel seeds. Cook until meat is brown and crumbled.
5. Remove from heat and add zucchini and cream, stirring to mix thoroughly.
6. Fold sheets of phyllo dough in half three times so each will fit in the tart cups. Place two in each cup, overlapping so that each edge of the tart cup is covered.
7. Brush dough with melted butter.
8. Divided meat mixture evenly among the tart cups.
9. Blend cheeses and top each tart cup with an equal amount of cheese.
10. Bake for about 20 minutes, until dough edges are crisp and cheese is melted and bubbly.

Miniature Zucchini Wellingtons

- 16 sheets phyllo dough, thawed
- 2 tablespoons plus 1 teaspoon butter
- 2 medium zucchini, cut into eight equal pieces each
- Two cups button mushrooms, finely diced
- 2 gloves garlic, minced
- Two cups portabella mushroom caps, finely diced
- 1 cup mozzarella cheese
- Melted butter for basting
- Beef dipping sauce

1. Melt 2 tablespoons butter in a saucepan and add garlic and diced mushrooms. Salt to taste and cook until lightly browned and tender. Let cool.
2. Melt 1 teaspoon of butter in a saucepan and add zucchini slices. Sauté until slightly tender.
3. Fold phyllo dough into thirds and place a slice of zucchini at the end, followed by a spoonful of mushroom mixture and a pinch of cheese.
4. Roll up dough into a cigar-shaped cylinder and baste with melted butter.
5. Bake in a 325 degree oven for 20 minutes until browned and crispy.
6. Serve with Beef Dipping Sauce.

Beef Dipping Sauce: Melt 1 tablespoon butter into a small saucepan and add 1 clove smashed garlic and 1 tablespoon flour. Cook about 1 minute. Add 1 cup of beef stock or consommé and a dash of Worcestershire sauce. Cook over medium heat until thick and bubbly, stirring constantly.

SOUPS

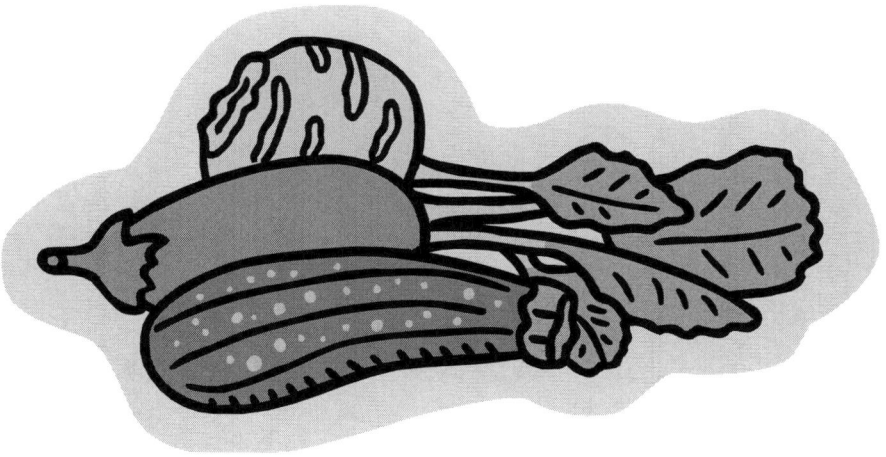

Bring a bit of warmth to any meal with creamy, meaty or light soups that will easily be the star
of any meal.

Creamy Zucchini Soup

- **Three cups diced zucchini**
- **1 teaspoon Italian seasoning**
- **Two cups chicken stock**
- **1 cup half and half**
- **1 tablespoon flour**
- **1 tablespoon butter**
- **1/4 teaspoon sea salt**
- **1/4 teaspoon black pepper**

1. Sauté diced zucchini in olive oil until tender.
2. Blend with ½ cup chicken stock until liquefied.
3. Mix remaining stock, half and half, flour, butter and seasonings in a saucepan.
4. Add zucchini and simmer over low heat until bubbly.

Veggie Chicken Soup

- **1 tablespoon olive oil**
- **2 carrots, matchstick sliced**
- **1 yellow onion, thinly sliced**
- **1 cup cabbage, finely sliced**
- **1 zucchini, matchstick sliced**
- **3 cloves garlic, minced**
- **Six cups chicken stock**
- **2 teaspoons soy sauce**
- **2 chicken breasts, cooked and shredded**
- **¼ cup cilantro leaves**

1. Heat olive oil over medium heat in a medium stock kettle. Add carrots, onion and cabbage and cook until onion is translucent and carrots are beginning to tenderize. Add zucchini and garlic and cook two minutes more.
2. Add chicken broth, shredded chicken and soy sauce and cook until heated through.
3. Add cilantro leaves and cook for a few minutes and serve.

Roasted Vegetable Soup

- 2 baking potatoes, peeled and cut into chunks
- 2 carrots, peeled and cut into pieces
  2 zucchini, sliced in half and cut into chunks
- 1 yellow onion, cut into pieces
- 1 green bell pepper, halved and seeded
- 2 cups assorted mushrooms
- 3 small green hot peppers, sliced and seeded
- 4 cloves garlic
- Olive oil
- Salt and pepper to taste
- 3 cups chicken stock
- 1 cup cream
- 1 teaspoon Italian seasoning
- Dash cayenne pepper

1. Preheat oven to 375 degrees.
2. Prepare vegetables and place on a cookie sheet or pizza pan in a single layer.
3. Brush with olive oil and sprinkle with salt and pepper to taste.
4. Roast vegetables in oven until tender and caramelized. Check them often, as some veggies will be soft and caramelized before others.
5. As vegetables become ready, toss them, a few at a time, in a blender with some of the chicken stock, blending until smooth and creamy.
6. When all the vegetables are blended into the chicken stock, mix them together into a large saucepan.
7. Add cream, Italian seasoning and cayenne pepper and cook over low heat until warm and bubbly.

California Vegetable Cheese Soup

- 4 carrots, peeled and sliced
- ½ head cauliflower, cut into small pieces
- 1 stalk broccoli florets, cut into small pieces.
- 1 medium onion, sliced
- 10 ounces ground turkey breast
- 2 medium zucchini, shredded
- 4 tablespoons butter
- 4 tablespoons flour
- 3 cups milk
- 2 cups shredded cheddar cheese
- 1 cup shredded process American cheese
- 2 tablespoons shredded Asiago cheese
- 16 ounces chicken stock
- Salt and pepper to taste

1. Steam carrots, cauliflower and broccoli until tender; set aside.
2. Sauté onion in a bit of olive oil or butter until translucent and almost tender. Add ground turkey and zucchini and cook until turkey is browned.
3. Meanwhile, melt butter in a medium saucepan and add flour. Stir until smooth.
4. Add milk and cook until thickened and bubbly,
5. Add cheeses one cup at a time, stirring until melted.
6. Transfer to a soup pot and add chicken stock.
7. Add steamed vegetables and turkey mixture and simmer for 10 or 14 minutes on low heat so flavors can blend together.
8. Season with salt and pepper and serve with crusty bread.

Mexican Tortilla Soup

- 1 onion, diced
- 1 green bell pepper, diced
- 2 small hot peppers, diced
- 1 medium zucchini, shredded
- 4 cups chicken broth
- 2 shredded chicken breasts
- 1 15-ounce can petite diced tomatoes
- 1 cup frozen corn
- 2 teaspoon ground cumin
- 1 teaspoon salt
- ½ cup cilantro leaves
- Tortilla strips

1. Line the bottom of a soup pot with olive oil and sauce onions, bell pepper and hot peppers until tender.
2. Add zucchini shreds and cook about five minutes.
3. Add chicken broth, shredded chicken, tomatoes, frozen corn, ground cumin and salt.
4. Bring to a boil and reduce heat, simmering for about 30 minutes for flavors to meld.
5. Just before serving, add cilantro leaves and top with tortilla strips.

BREADS

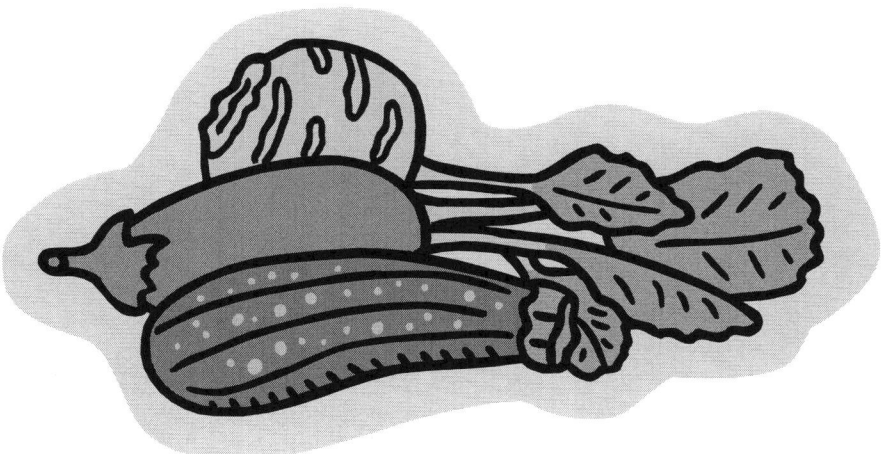

Zucchini amps up the taste and texture of breads and muffins, resulting in sweet, moist and delicious treats.

Sweet Spiced Zucchini Bread

- **Two cups flour**
- **1 teaspoon salt**
- **1 teaspoon baking soda**
- **1 teaspoon baking powder**
- **2 teaspoons cinnamon**
- **½ teaspoon nutmeg**
- **½ teaspoon allspice**
- **2 ¼ cups sugar**
- **1 cup oil**
- **3 eggs**
- **2 teaspoons vanilla**
- **2 cups grated zucchini**

1. Preheat oven to 325 degrees.
2. Butter and flour two 8x4 bread pans and set aside.
3. Mix dry ingredients in a bowl and set aside.
4. Cream together eggs, sugar, oil and vanilla until well blended.
5. Slowly add dry ingredients and beat well.
6. Stir in zucchini until well combined.
7. Pour batter into prepared pans.
8. Bake at 325 degrees for 45 to 60 minutes, until a toothpick inserted into the center comes out clean.
9. Cool before removing from pans.

Lemon Zucchini Bread

- 1 ¾ cup flour
- 1 cup sugar
- 2 teaspoons baking powder
- ¼ teaspoon salt
- 1 beaten egg
- 1 cup milk
- ½ cup finely grated zucchini
- ¼ cup oil
- 2 tablespoons lemon juice
- 1 teaspoon lemon zest
- Lemon Glaze (recipe below)

1. Preheat oven to 350 degrees.
2. Butter and flour one 8x4 inch bread pan and set aside.
3. Mix flour, sugar, baking powder and salt together in a mixing bowl; set aside.
4. Mix egg, butter, zucchini, oil, lemon juice and lemon zest in a medium bowl.
5. Add liquid mixture to flour mixture and mix until blended.
6. Pour into prepared pan.
7. Bake in a 350 degree oven for 50 minutes or until lightly golden.
8. Top with Lemon Glaze.

Lemon Glaze: Mix 1 cup confectioners' sugar with 2 tablespoons lemon juice and mix until smooth. Pour evenly over baked Lemon Zucchini Bread.

Chocolate Zucchini Quick Bread

- 1 ¾ cup flour
- 1 cup sugar
- ¼ cup cocoa
- 2 teaspoons baking powder
- ¼ teaspoon salt
- 1 beaten egg
- 1 cup shredded zucchini
- ¼ cup oil
- 1 cup milk
- 1 ounce bittersweet chocolate

1. Preheat oven to 350 degrees.
2. Grease and flour and 8x4 inch bread pan; set aside.
3. Mix flour, sugar, cocoa, baking powder and salt into a mixing bowl; set aside.
4. Mix egg, zucchini and oil together.
5. Melt chocolate into milk over low heat in a medium saucepan; add to egg mixture.
6. Pour liquid mixture into flour mixture and mix until well blended.
7. Pour into prepared pan.
8. Bake in a 350 degree oven for 50 minutes or until a toothpick inserted near the center comes out clean.

Spiced Blueberry Pie Muffins

- **2 cups flour**
- **1/2 cup sugar**
- **2 teaspoons baking powder**
- **1 teaspoon cinnamon**
- **½ teaspoon Chinese Five Spice**
- **¼ teaspoon salt**
- **2 eggs, beaten**
- **½ cup finely shredded zucchini**
- **¾ cup blueberry pie filling**
- **¾ cup milk**
- **½ cup fresh blueberries**
- **¼ cup vegetable oil**
- **1 teaspoons vanilla**

1. Preheat oven to 400 degrees.
2. Mix flour, sugar, baking powder and cinnamon; set aside.
3. Mix together eggs, zucchini, pie filling, milk, Blueberries oil and vanilla, stirring well.
4. Add wet ingredients to the flour mixture and stir just until moist.
5. Spoon batter into paper lined muffin cups and sprinkle lightly with sugar.
6. Bake about 18 minutes, until muffins just start to brown.
7. Makes 12 muffins.

Chocolate Chip Muffins

- **2 cups flour**
- **1/2 cup sugar**
- **2 teaspoons baking powder**
- **¼ teaspoon salt**
- **2 eggs, beaten**
- **½ cup finely shredded zucchini**
- **¾ cup milk**
- **½ cup chocolate chips**
- **¼ cup vegetable oil**
- **2 teaspoons vanilla**

1. Preheat oven to 400 degrees.
2. Mix flour, sugar, baking powder and salt; set aside.
3. Mix together eggs, zucchini, milk, chocolate chips, oil and vanilla, stirring well.
4. Add wet ingredients to the flour mixture and stir just until moist.
5. Spoon batter into paper lined muffin cups and sprinkle lightly with sugar.
6. Bake about 18 minutes, until muffins just start to brown.
7. Makes 12 muffins.

Lemon Poppy Seed Muffins

- 2 cups flour
- 1/2 cup sugar
- 1 tablespoon poppy seeds
- 2 teaspoons baking powder
- ¼ teaspoon salt
- 1 egg, beaten
- ½ cup finely shredded zucchini
- ¾ cup milk
- ¼ cup vegetable oil
- 3 tablespoons lemon juice
- 2 teaspoons lemon zest

1. Lemon Glaze (recipe follows)
2. Preheat oven to 400 degrees.
3. Mix flour, sugar, baking powder, salt and poppy seeds; set aside.
4. Mix together egg, zucchini, milk, oil, lemon juice and lemon zest, stirring well.
5. Add wet ingredients to the flour mixture and stir just until moist.
6. Spoon batter into paper lined muffin cups and sprinkle lightly with sugar.
7. Bake about 18 minutes, until muffins just start to brown.
8. When muffins are cool, frost with Lemon Glaze.

Lemon Glaze: Mix together ½ cup powdered sugar and 1 tablespoon lemon juice until smooth and creamy. Add more lemon juice if needed.

Oatmeal Zucchini Muffins

- **1 cup rolled oats**
- **1 cup buttermilk**
- **1 medium zucchini, shredded**
- **1 cup flour**
- **1 ½ teaspoon baking soda**
- **1 teaspoon cinnamon**
- **½ teaspoon baking soda**
- **¼ teaspoon nutmeg**
- **2 eggs, beaten**
- **½ cup packed brown sugar**
- **2 tablespoons vegetable oil**

1. Preheat oven to 400 degrees.
2. Mix oats, buttermilk and zucchini together; set aside.
3. Sift together flour, baking powder, baking soda, cinnamon and nutmeg.
4. Stir eggs, oil and brown sugar into oatmeal mixture.
5. Add wet ingredients to flour mixture and stir just until moist.
6. Bake in a 400 degree oven for 18 to 20 minutes.
7. Makes 12 muffins.

Spicy Zucchini Cornbread

- 1 cup yellow cornmeal
- 1 cup all-purpose flour
- ¼ cup sugar
- 1 tablespoon baking powder
- 1 teaspoon salt
- ½ teaspoon red pepper flakes
- 2 eggs
- 1 cup milk
- 1 cup corn
- 1 medium zucchini, shredded
- 2 tablespoons melted butter

1. Preheat oven to 400 degrees.
2. Mix cornmeal, flour, sugar, baking powder, salt and red pepper flakes; set aside.
3. Beat eggs and add milk, blending until mixed well.
4. Add wet ingredients to dry ingredients and stir until just mixed.
5. Add corn, zucchini and melted butter, mixing well.
6. Pour mixture into a buttered muffin pans and bake for about 15 minutes, until muffins are browned and edges are crispy.
7. Makes about 12.

Savory Zucchini Multigrain Bread

- 1 ¼ cup water
- 2 tablespoons butter, softened
- 2 ¾ teaspoons yeast
- 1 ¼ cup whole wheat flour
- ½ teaspoon salt
- 1 cup shredded zucchini
- ½ cup oatmeal
- ¼ cup packed brown sugar
- 2 tablespoons flax seed
- 2 cups all-purpose flour
- 1 ¼ cup whole wheat flour

1. Warm water to about 110 degrees. Add melted butter and yeast, stirring with a wooden spoon to mix well.
2. Add whole wheat flour and salt and beat with a hand mixer until well blended.
3. Add zucchini, oatmeal, brown sugar and flax seed and mix until well blended.
4. Stir in about a cup of flour with a wooden spoon, adding more until it is too difficult to stir.
5. Turn the dough out onto a floured surface and knead in the remaining flour, adding more if the dough feels sticky.
6. Cover with plastic wrap and let rise until it is doubled in size.
7. Punch it down and gently shape it into two round loaves, than place it on two greased baking sheets. Cover loosely with plastic wrap and let rise until loaves are doubled in size.
8. Bake in a 375 degree oven until bread sounds hollow when tapped, about 35 to 40 minutes.

FOR BREAD MACHINE: Pour wet ingredients into bread machine pan. Add dry ingredients except for yeast, substituting bread flour for all-purpose flour. Make a well in the flour and add yeast. Bake in bread machine according to instructions.

SANDWICHES

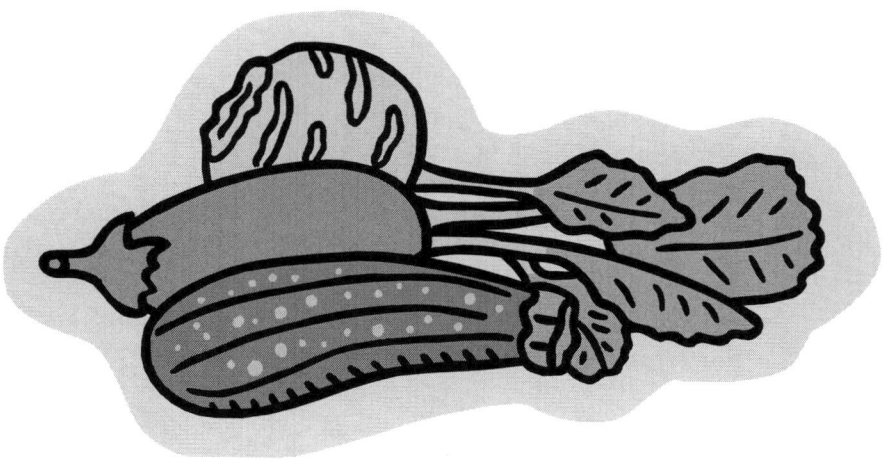

From tender zucchini slices hot off the grill to marinated strips of the versatile veggie, these sandwiches will make a quick, tasty meal.

Mega Pizza Roll

- 1 ½ pounds fresh pizza dough
- 8 ounces Italian sausage, cooked and crumbled
- 8 ounces shredded mozzarella cheese
- ½ yellow onion, finely chopped
- ½ green bell pepper, finely chopped
- 1 small zucchini, thinly sliced
- 1 8-ounce can Italian seasoned pizza sauce

1. Preheat oven to 375 degrees.
2. Sauté sausage in a little bit of olive oil in a medium saucepan until crumbled and browned.
3. Roll pizza dough out on a pizza pan.
4. Spread sauce evenly over dough.
5. Sprinkle with onion, green pepper, zucchini slices, sausage and cheese.
6. Gently roll dough as if making a jelly roll.
7. Bake in a 375 degree oven for 35 t- 40 minutes or until crust is browned.
8. Cut into slices and serve.

Marinated Vegetable Sandwiches

- **1 red bell pepper, sliced**
- **1 green bell pepper, sliced**
- **1 small onion, sliced**
- **1 medium zucchini, halved and sliced into julienne slices, seeds discarded**
- **1 bottle Italian dressing and marinade**
- **4 Romaine lettuce leaves**
- **4 to 8 slices provolone cheese**
- **4 sub buns**

1. Slice vegetables and pour Italian dressing over them. Chill for at least two hours.
2. When ready to serve, place a lettuce leaf on the bottom of a toasted sub bun.

Grilled Zucchini Sandwich
with Caramelized Onions

- 1 large baguette, toasted
- 2 medium zucchini, thinly sliced lengthwise
- 2 teaspoons olive oil
- 1 tablespoon butter
- 1 teaspoon sugar
- 2 large onions, sliced
- 1 ripe tomato, thinly sliced
- Two Romaine lettuce leaves
- 2 or three slices smoked Provolone cheese
- 1 tablespoon mayonnaise
- 1 teaspoon spicy brown mustard
- Dash freshly ground black pepper

1. Melt butter in a large frying pan and add onions and sugar. Salt to taste and season and cook over medium heat until onions are tender and caramelized. Set aside.
2. Lightly baste zucchini slices with olive oil and grill them until gently charred and tender.
3. Mix mayonnaise, mustard and black pepper. Spread on one side of the baguette.
4. Top with lettuce, zucchini slices, tomato and onions.
5. Finish with cheese and broil until cheese is slightly melted.

Sloppy Joes

- 1 small onion, chopped
- 1 small green pepper, chopped
- 1 pound ground beef or turkey
- 2 cloves garlic
- Pinch red pepper flakes
- 1 medium zucchini, shredded
- 1 8-ounce can tomato sauce
- 1 ½ teaspoons chili powder
- 1 teaspoon Worcestershire sauce
- ½ teaspoon salt
- ¼ teaspoon garlic powder

1. Coat a sauté pan with olive oil and cook onion and green pepper until onion in translucent.
2. Add ground meat, garlic and red pepper flakes and cook until meat is browned.
3. Add zucchini, tomato sauce, chili powder, Worcestershire sauce, salt and garlic powder and bring to a simmer.
4. Cook for about 15 minutes to allow flavors to meld. Serve on toasted buns.

Meatball Sub Sandwiches

- 2 slices bacon, crumbled
- 1 small onion, minced
- 4 cloves garlic, minced
- 1 pound ground beef
- 1 small zucchini, shredded
- 1 egg
- ¼ cup bread crumbs
- ¼ cup Parmesan cheese
- ½ teaspoon salt
- ¼ teaspoon black pepper
- 1 cup tomato sauce
- **Four slices mozzarella or provolone cheese**
- **Four sub buns**

1. Preheat oven to 350 degrees.
2. Cook bacon and set aside, reserving bacon fat.
3. Add onion to hot pan, cooking in bacon fat for about five minutes. Add garlic and cook about one minute more.
4. Mix bacon, ground beef, zucchini, egg, bread crumbs, Parmesan cheese, salt and pepper. Add onion and garlic and mix until well blended.
5. Shape mixture into meatballs and bake in a 350-degree oven for about 30 minutes, until meatballs are browned and cooked through.
6. Toss meatballs with tomato sauce and arrange on toasted sub buns.
7. Cover with cheese slices and broil until cheese is melted and bubbly.

Serves four.

BREAKFAST MENU

Zucchini amps up the taste and texture of breads and muffins, resulting in sweet, moist and delicious treats.

Buttermilk Zucchini Pancakes

- **1 cup all-purpose flour**
- **1 tablespoon sugar**
- **1 teaspoon baking powder**
- **½ teaspoon baking soda**
- **½ teaspoon salt**
- **1 beaten egg**
- **1 cup buttermilk**
- **½ cup finely shredded zucchini**
- **2 tablespoons cooking oil**

1. Mix flour, sugar, baking soda, baking powder and salt together; set aside.
2. Beat egg, milk, zucchini and oil together.
3. Pour egg mixture into the center of the flour mixture and stir until blended.
4. Cook over hot griddle until both sides are browned.
5. Serve with syrup and butter.
6. *Serves three.*

Italian Zucchini Strata

- 4 English muffins
- Six slices bacon, cooked and crumbled
- 2 small zucchini, diced
- 1 cup baby spinach leaves
- 1 small sweet onion, finely diced
- 4 ounces shredded cheese, a mix of Fontina, Parmesan and aged white Cheddar
- 4 eggs
- 1 ¼ cup milk
- ¼ cup sour cream
- 1/8 teaspoon black pepper

1. Cut English muffins into bite-size pieces and spread half of them out in a greased, two-quart baking dish.
2. Sprinkle muffins with bacon, zucchini, spinach leaves, onion and cheese.
3. Top with remaining English muffins.
4. Beat eggs and add milk and sour cream, as well as black pepper, whisking until well blended.
5. Pour evenly over the top of the muffins. Cover and chill up to 24 hours.
6. Bake in a 325 degree oven for 60 to 65 minutes, until a knife inserted in the center comes out clean.
7. Allow strata to rest 10 minutes before serving.

Zucchini & Spinach Frittata

- **6 large eggs**
- **½ cup grated Parmesan cheese**
- **2 slices bacon, cooked and crumbled**
- **½ teaspoon salt**
- **¼ teaspoon fresh ground black pepper**
- **2 tablespoons olive oil**
- **1 small onion, finely diced**
- **1 small zucchini, diced**
- **1 cup baby spinach leaves, sliced**
- **Preheat oven to 400 degrees.**

1. Whisk together eggs, cheese, bacon, salt and pepper; set aside.
2. In a medium cast-iron skillet, heat olive oil over medium heat. Add onion and cook until brown, about 5 minutes.
3. Add zucchini and cook another two minutes,
4. Top with spinach leaves and pour egg mixture over the top, reducing heat to low and cooking about 7 minutes.
5. Place frittata in the oven to finish and bake until light brown, about 5 minutes.

Serves four to six.

Breakfast Skillet

- **3 cups shredded hash browns, thawed**
- **1 egg white**
- **1 small onion, diced**
- **1 tablespoon minced shallot**
- **1 medium zucchini, shredded**
- **5 eggs, beaten**
- **½ cup diced ham**
- **½ cup shredded cheddar cheese**

1. Preheat oven to 350 degrees.
2. Mix hash browns and egg white and press into a pie plate. Bake for about 15 to 20 minutes, until edges begin to brown.
3. Melt 1 teaspoon butter in a sauté pan and cook onion and shallot until onion is soft and translucent. Add zucchini and cook one minute more.
4. Mix eggs, ham and cheese and add onion mixture.
5. Pour into the hash brown shell and bake about 30 minutes until set.

Zucchini & Tomato Pie

- 2 ripe heirloom tomatoes, sliced
- 1 medium zucchini, sliced
- 1 yellow squash, sliced
- ½ cup milk
- 1 cup shredded Fontina or Gruyere cheese
- 2 green onions, thinly sliced
- ½ teaspoon salt
- ¼ teaspoon pepper
- 2 slices bacon, cooked and crumbled
- ¼ cup grated Parmesan cheese
- 1 deep- dish pie crust

1. Slice tomatoes and place them on paper towels to absorb excess moisture.
2. Slice zucchini and yellow squash slices and place them in a colander. Salt them liberally and allow them to rest for 30 minutes to an hour to drain excess water.
3. Mix milk, cheese, onions, salt and pepper. Add bacon.
4. Pat squash slices dry and layer them on the bottom of the pie crust, alternating colors.
5. Pour cheese mixture over the top of the squash slices.
6. Top with tomato slices.
7. Bake in a 375-degree oven for 30 minutes.
8. Top with Parmesan cheese and bake 15 to 20 minutes more, until a knife inserted in the center comes out clean.
9. Let stand for about 10 minutes before serving.

Serves six.

SALADS

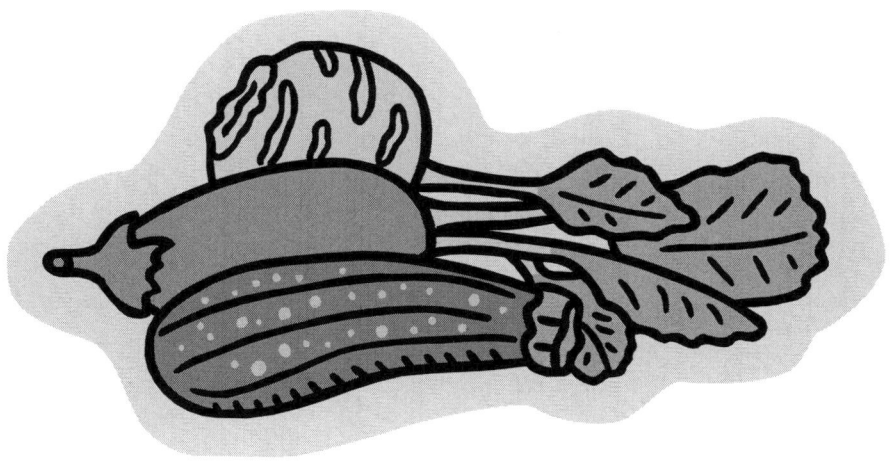

Light summer meals start with
fresh-from-the-garden veggies, the stars
of these light main dish and side salads.

Zucchini Pasta Salad

- 1 box tri-colored rotini pasta
- 1 green bell pepper, diced
- 1 purple onion, diced
- 2 medium zucchini, diced
- 2 14.5-ounce cans Italian-style chunk tomatoes
1. Cook pasta according to package instructions, set aside.
2. Coat a sauté pan with olive oil and sauté onion and bell pepper until almost tender.
3. Add zucchini and cook, covered, until zucchini chunks are tender but still firm.
4. Mix pasta and veggies together, then toss with tomatoes.
5. Serve hot or cold.

Zucchini Citrus Salad

- 3 medium zucchini
- 1 small can mandarin oranges
- 1 tablespoon orange juice
- 1 teaspoon orange zest
- 1 tablespoon extra-virgin olive oil
- 2 tablespoons fresh basil leaves
1. Peel zucchini and cut into cubes.
2. Add mandarin oranges
3. Toss with olive oil, orange juice and orange zest.
4. Add torn basil leaves and serve freshly chilled.

Grilled Zucchini & Steak Salad

- 1 large steak for grilling
- Six cups baby spinach
- 2 medium zucchini, sliced lengthwise
- Olive oil for basting
- ½ small red onion, thinly sliced
- About 10 cherry tomatoes, cut in half
- Handful of button mushrooms, sliced
- Crumbled blue cheese

1. Season steak with salt and pepper and grill to desired level of doneness; set aside to rest.
2. Brush zucchini slices with olive oil and grill until tender, about 5 minutes. Cut into bite-size pieces.
3. Divide spinach into two bowls and toss with red onion, tomatoes and mushrooms.
4. Slice steak into bite-size pieces and divide between the two bowls.
5. Add zucchini and toss well.
6. Top with blue cheese and choice of dressing.

Caprese Salad with Grilled Zucchini

- **2 medium zucchini, sliced lengthwise**
- **2 large vine-ripened tomatoes**
- **8 slices fresh mozzarella cheese**
- **1 cup fresh basil leaves, sliced into a chiffonade**
- **Olive oil for basting and to finish**

1. Brush zucchini slices with olive oil and sprinkle with salt to taste.
2. Grill until zucchini is tender, about 5 minutes, then cut slices in half.
3. Slice tomatoes and begin layering ingredients, tomato, zucchini and cheese, either in a round or rectangular format.
4. Top with basil, salt and pepper.
5. Drizzle with olive oil just before serving.

Spring Zucchini and Orzo Salad

- 8 ounces orzo pasta, cooked as per package instructions
- 2 or 3 medium zucchini, diced
- 1 cup fresh or frozen baby peas
- 1 cup spinach, cut in a chiffonade
- 2 tablespoons olive oil
- 2 tablespoons lemon juice
- ¼ teaspoon salt
- ¼ cup shredded Parmesan cheese, plus more for topping

1. Cook pasta and set it aside.
2. Coat a sauté pan with olive oil and gently sauté zucchini cubes until they begin to tenderize.
3. Add salt and pepper to taste.
4. Toss in peas and spinach and cook until spinach slightly wilts.
5. Toss with orzo, olive oil, lemon juice and ¼ cup of Parmesan cheese
6. Serve topped with shredded cheese.

Creamy Veggie Coleslaw

- 1 small head cabbage
- 2 large carrots, peeled
- 1 stalk celery
- 1 medium zucchini
- Two green onions
- 1 cup mayonnaise
- 2 tablespoons sugar
- 1 tablespoon balsamic vinegar

1. Salt and pepper to taste
2. Shred vegetables in a food processor.
3. Mix mayonnaise, sugar, vinegar and salt and pepper, stirring until well blended.
4. Pour over shredded vegetables and mix well. Chill until serving.

Marinated Veggie Salad

- **2 bunches romaine hearts, torn**
- **1 15-ounce can chickpeas, rinsed and drained**
- **1 medium zucchini, diced**
- **1 cup cherry tomatoes, halved**
- **1 8-ounce jar marinated artichoke hearts, drained**
- **1 3.5-ounce can sliced black olives**
- **Italian dressing and marinade**

1. Mix chickpeas, zucchini, tomatoes, artichoke hearts and black olives.
2. Toss with Italian dressing and chill at least four hours before serving.
3. Serve over torn romaine leaves.

SIDE DISHES

Succulent zucchini is a super side,
from sautéed with fresh herbs
to baked with creamy, luscious, gooey
cheeses.

Stuffed Zucchini

- 2 medium zucchini
- ½ cup onion, chopped
- ½ cup tomato, peeled and seeded
- 1 cob corn
- 1 tablespoon olive oil
- ½ cup bread crumbs
- ½ cup shredded Italian cheese
- Pinch Italian seasoning
- 1 tablespoon melted butter
- 1 tablespoon shredded Italian cheese
- Salt and pepper to taste

1. Preheat oven to 325 degrees F.
2. Slice zucchini in half lengthwise, removing the seeds from one side and dicing the other.
3. Sauté diced zucchini, onion, corn and tomato in olive oil until tender.
4. Mix with bread crumbs, cheese and butter until well blended. Stuff into hollowed zucchini and top with remaining cheese.
5. Bake for 45 minutes or until cheese is melted and bubbly.

Parmesan Baked Zucchini

- **2 medium zucchini, halved**
- **Olive oil**
- **Salt and pepper to taste**
- **2 tablespoons grated Parmesan cheese**

1. Preheat oven to 350 degrees F.
2. Slice zucchini in half lengthwise.
3. Brush each half with olive oil; dust with salt and pepper.
4. Top with Parmesan cheese and bake in a 350 degree oven about one hour, until zucchini is tender and cheese is toasted.

Grilled Zucchini

- **3 medium zucchini, sliced lengthwise, ends removed**
- **2 tablespoons olive oil**
- **Salt and pepper to taste**

1. With a basting brush, brush both sides of zucchini slices with olive oil.
2. Season with salt and pepper and cook on a hot grill until tender, about 5 to 10 minutes, turning halfway through.

Layered Zucchini & Tomatoes

- 2 medium zucchini, sliced into thin rounds
- 1 yellow squash, sliced
- 2 heirloom tomatoes, sliced
- 1 cup shredded Italian cheese (a blend of Parmesan, Romano, Mozzarella and Asiago)
- ¼ cup torn basil leaves

1. Salt zucchini slices and place them in a colander for about an hour, allowing excess moisture to drain. Pat dry between two layers of paper towel.
2. Slice tomatoes and allow them to rest for a few minutes on paper towels.
3. Preheat oven to 350 degrees F.
4. Arrange a single layer of zucchini on the bottom of a glass casserole, overlapping to make a ring, sprinkling with salt and pepper to taste.
5. Top with a layer of tomato slices, a third of the basil and ¼ cup of cheese.
6. Continue layering with a center layer of yellow squash, followed by tomato slices, basil and cheese. The third layer will start with zucchini and end with the remaining cheese.
7. Bake in a 350 degree oven for about 30 minutes, until cheese is bubbly and bread crumbs are browned.

Zucchini-Potato Hash Browns

- **1 medium zucchini, shredded**
- **1 medium baking potato, shredded**
- **½ yellow onion, shredded**
- **½ cup flour**
- **1 beaten egg**
- **Salt and pepper to taste**

1. Place shredded zucchini into a colander and salt generously. Set aside for about 30 minutes to allow extra moisture to be released. Pat zucchini dry with a paper towel.
2. Mix zucchini, potato and onion together.
3. Add flour, egg, salt and pepper and mix well.
4. Shape into patties and fry in hot oil until browned and crispy.

Zucchini and Cheese Soufflé

- **4 eggs, separated**
- **1 cup finely shredded zucchini**
- **1 cup milk**
- **¼ cup butter**
- **¼ cup flour**
- **2 cups shredded cheese, a mix of Colby, smoked cheddar and Swiss**
- **½ teaspoon dry mustard**

1. Preheat oven to 350 degrees.
2. Beat egg yolks until well mixed; add zucchini. Set aside.
3. Melt butter in a medium saucepan, add flour, dry mustard and black pepper and mix until smooth.
4. Add milk and stir over medium heat until thick and bubbly.
5. Add cheese slowly until melted.
6. Add cheese sauce to egg mixture and set aside.
7. Whip egg whites until stiff peaks form.
8. Folk cheese mixture and egg whites together gently and pour into a soufflé pan or glass baking dish.
9. Bake at 350 degrees for about 50 minutes or until a knife inserted into the center comes out clean.

Sautéed Zucchini in Cheese Sauce

- 2 medium zucchini, thinly sliced
- ½ yellow onion, thinly sliced
- 1 tablespoon butter
- 1 tablespoon flour
- ¾ cup milk
- ¾ cup shredded sharp Cheddar Cheese
- 4 ounces processed American cheese, cubed
- 1 tablespoon shredded Asiago cheese
- Salt and pepper to taste

1. Sauté sliced zucchini and onion in a skillet until tender.
2. Meanwhile, melt butter in a small saucepan. Add flour and mix until blended.
3. Add milk and a dash of black pepper and cook, stirring constantly, until thick and bubbly.
4. Slowly add cheese and stir until melted.
5. Pour cheese sauce over zucchini mixture and stir well.

Zucchini-Spinach Sauté

- 1 teaspoon olive oil
- 1 teaspoon butter
- 2 medium zucchini, shredded
- 4 cups baby spinach
- 2 tablespoons shredded Parmesan
- Salt and pepper to taste

1. Heat olive oil and butter in a saucepan over medium heat.
2. Add zucchini and sauté until shreds are tender but not browned.
3. Add spinach and toss until spinach is wilted.
4. Season with salt and pepper and add shredded cheese.

Ratatouille

- 2 tablespoons olive oil
- 1 medium onion, finely chopped
- ½ green bell pepper, finely chopped
- 8 ounces tomato sauce
- 2 cloves minced garlic
- 1 tablespoon fresh chopped basil
- 1 medium zucchini, diced
- 1 yellow squash, diced
- 1 baby or Japanese eggplant, diced
- **Salt and pepper to taste**

1. Preheat oven to 350 degrees.
2. Sauté onion and bell pepper in olive oil until slightly tender. Add tomato sauce, garlic and basil and simmer about 10 minutes.
3. Toss diced zucchini, squash and eggplant with sauce and season with salt and pepper to taste.
4. Pour mixture into a glass baking dish.
5. Bake for about 45 minutes, until vegetables are tender.

Zucchini Lasagna

- Two large zucchini, julienne sliced lengthwise
- 1 tablespoon butter
- 3 cups sliced button or baby portabella mushrooms
- 2 gloves garlic, minced
- 1/8 teaspoon salt
- Dash red pepper flakes
- 1 tablespoon flour
- ½ cup chicken stock
- ½ cup heavy cream
- 1 cup ricotta cheese
- ¼ cup cream cheese
- ¼ teaspoon Italian seasoning
- 1 cup chopped spinach
- 1 cup shredded mozzarella cheese
- 2 tablespoons Parmesan cheese

1. Slice zucchini and sprinkle with salt, setting them aside to drain off excess liquid.
2. Melt butter in a large saucepan and add mushrooms, garlic, salt and red pepper flakes Sauté on low heat until mushrooms are tender.
3. Add 1 tablespoon of flour and cook for about 1 minute. Add chicken stock and cream, cook until sauce is thick and bubbly.
4. Mix together ricotta, cream cheese, Italian seasoning and chopped spinach.
5. Pat zucchini slices dry.
6. To begin layering your lasagna, spread a few tablespoons of mushroom sauce on the bottom of a casserole. Top with slices of zucchini layered as you would lasagna noodles.
7. Top zucchini with a third of the cheese and spinach mixture, spreading it out evenly. Sprinkle with ¼ cup of mozzarella cheese.
8. Spread about 1/3 of the remaining mushroom sauce over the mozzarella and repeat the process, finishing with mozzarella and Parmesan cheese.
9. Bake in a 350 degree oven for about 45 minutes, until cheese is browned and bubbly.

Creamy Spiced Zucchini

- 2 slices bacon, chopped, fried crisp
- Pinch red pepper flakes
- 1 tablespoon flour
- 1 clove garlic, minced
- 1 cup milk
- 2 zucchini, sliced thin

1. Fry bacon, reserving grease and removing bacon to a paper towel to drain. Add red pepper flakes, flour and garlic, cooking about one or two minutes, stirring constantly.
2. Add milk and cook until sauce is thick and bubbly.
3. Add zucchini and cook until soft and tender.
4. Add bacon and serve warm.

Italian Zucchini

- 2 medium zucchini, shredded
- ¼ cup fresh basil, finely chopped
- 2 teaspoons extra virgin olive oil
- 1 teaspoon Italian seasoning
- ¼ cup shredded Parmesan cheese

1. Salt shredded zucchini generously and set aside for about 30 minutes, patting dry with a paper towel before cooking.
2. Heat a large sauté pan and add Italian seasoning, toasting slightly.
3. Add olive oil, zucchini and basil. Cook until zucchini is tender and basil is wilted.

Zucchini in Brown Butter & Sage Sauce

- **2 medium zucchini, shredded**
- **2 tablespoons butter**
- **2 tablespoons fresh sage, minced**
- **Salt and pepper to taste**
- **2 tablespoons fresh grated Parmesan cheese**
1. Shred zucchini and set aside.
2. Melt butter in a sauté pan over medium heat until milk solids separate and butter begins to turn a warm caramel color. Be careful not to burn it.
3. Add sage and stir until leaves are coated.
4. Add zucchini, season with salt and pepper to taste, and cook about three to five minutes.
5. Toss with cheese and serve.

Zucchini & Cauliflower Mash

- **½ head cauliflower, trimmed and cut into pieces**
- **3 medium zucchini, peeled and cut into 1-inch pieces**
- **2 tablespoons butter**
- **2 tablespoons heavy cream**
- **Salt and pepper to taste**
1. Steam zucchini and cauliflower until soft and completely tender.
2. Add butter, cream, salt and pepper and mash with a potato masher until smooth and creamy.

Scalloped Zucchini & Potatoes

- 2 cups frozen hash brown potatoes, thawed
- 2 medium zucchini, shredded
- 1 cup diced ham
- ½ tablespoons butter
- 2 tablespoons flour
- 2 cloves minced garlic
- 1 cup chicken broth
- ½ cup heavy cream
- ¼ teaspoon salt
- Dash white pepper
- ½ cup shredded cheddar cheese
- ¼ cup shredded Parmesan cheese

1. Salt shredded zucchini and set it aside for 15 minutes to allow moisture to escape. Squeeze excess water from the zucchini with a paper towel.
2. Place zucchini, shredded hash browns and diced ham in a casserole; set aside.
3. Preheat oven to 375 degrees.
4. Melt butter in a medium saucepan over medium heat. Add flour and cook for one or two minutes, stirring constantly.
5. Add broth, cream, salt and pepper and bring to a boil, then reduce heat and cook until mixture is thick and bubbly.
6. Add cheeses and stir until cheese is completely melted.
7. Pour sauce over zucchini, hash browns and ham
8. Bake in a 375 degree oven for 40 to 45 minutes, until top is slightly browned and cheese sauce is bubbly.

MAIN DISHES

Zucchini adds color, texture and flavor to these main-dish temptations, dishes that are easy to make and sure to please even fussy eaters.

Japanese Steakhouse Venison

- **4 cups brown rice as prepared from package instructions**
- **11/2 pounds venison or beef, cut into chunks**
- **1 large yellow onion, sliced**
- **2 tablespoons olive oil**
- **1 tablespoon butter**
- **2 medium zucchini, julienned**
- **White Sauce, recipe below**

1. Several hours before serving, mix sauce ingredients together until smooth; set aside.
2. Sauté onion in olive oil until it begins to become tender.
3. Add venison chunks and butter and cook until meat is only slightly pink.
4. Add zucchini, cover and simmer until zucchini is tender.
5. Serve over rice and drizzled with sauce.

White Sauce: Mix 1 ¼ cups mayonnaise, ¼ cup water, 1 tablespoon melted butter, 1 teaspoon tomato paste, 1 teaspoon garlic powder, ¼ teaspoon paprika, dash cayenne pepper. Chill for several hours before serving.
Serves four.

One-Pot Zucchini Casserole

- 1 pound ground venison or turkey
- 1 yellow onion, chopped
- 1 green bell pepper, diced
- 2 medium zucchini, sliced into thin rounds
- 1 14.5 ounce can Italian-seasoned tomato sauce
- 1 8-ounce package shredded mozzarella cheese

1. Brown ground venison or turkey breast along with onion and bell pepper in a little bit of olive oil until meat is no longer pink.
2. Add tomato sauce and zucchini slices, and cover, cooking until zucchini slices are tender, about 30 minutes.
3. Top with cheese and cook until cheese is melted and bubbly.
4. NOTE: Give this Mexican flair by adding a can of black beans, a cup of frozen corn and trading Italian tomatoes for chili-seasoned tomatoes. Top with tortilla strips.

Serves four.

Zucchini & Mushroom Meatloaf

- 1 pound ground chuck
- 1 large zucchini, grated
- 1 cup mushrooms, finely chopped
- 1 cup canned white beans
- ½ cup dry bread crumbs
- 1 egg
- 3 cloves garlic
- 1 teaspoon salt
- ½ teaspoon black pepper

1. Preheat oven to 350 degrees.
2. In a large bowl, mix together all ingredients until well blended.
3. Press into glass baking dish and bake about 60 minutes, until top of loaf is browned.

Veggie Stuffed Meatloaf

- **1 ½ pounds ground beef and pork**
- **1 medium zucchini, shredded**
- **½ medium yellow onion, finely chopped**
- **½ green bell pepper, finely chopped**
- **¾ cup dry bread crumbs**
- **½ cup milk**
- **2 eggs, beaten**
- **2 tablespoons ketchup**
- **1 tablespoon spicy mustard**
- **1 clove garlic, minced**
- **1 teaspoon salt**
- **1 teaspoon black pepper**
- **½ teaspoon ground cumin**

Preheat oven to 350 degrees.

1. Blend ground beef and pork together.
2. Mix eggs, milk, bread crumbs and spices.
3. Add to meat mixture and mix until well blended.
4. Bake in a 350 degree oven for an hour and 10 minutes, or until top of loaf is well browned.

Loaded Chicken Parmesan

1 pound chicken breasts, skinned and boned
1 jar spicy marinara sauce
1 yellow onion, chopped
1 green bell pepper, diced
1 medium zucchini, diced
1 package sliced mozzarella cheese
½ cup Italian seasoned bread crumbs
1 egg
¼ cup shredded Parmesan cheese

1. Preheat oven to 375 degrees.
2. Beat egg and add a little bit of water to make an egg wash.
3. Dry chicken breasts and dip first into egg wash, then bread crumbs, until well coated.
4. Fry in olive oil until both sides are browned and crunchy.
5. Place chicken breasts into baking pan and cover with mozzarella cheese, several slices per breast, then pour marinara sauce over the top.
6. Top with remaining mozzarella cheese and Parmesan.
7. Bake for about 45 minutes until cheese is browned and bubbly.
8. Serve over pasta.
9. *Serves four.*

Zucchini Parmesan

- 2 large zucchini, sliced into ¼-inch coins
- ¼ cup olive oil
- 1 egg, beaten
- 1 tablespoon milk
- ½ cup bread crumbs
- ½ cup flour
- ½ teaspoon Italian seasoning
- 1 ½ cups tomato sauce
- 1 cup mozzarella cheese
- 1 tablespoon fresh basil, torn
- ¼ cup Parmesan cheese, shredded

1. Slice zucchini and place them in a colander. Sprinkle with salt and allow them to rest for an hour so excess moisture is released.
2. Preheat oven to 375 degrees.
3. Heat olive oil in a sauté pan over medium heat.
4. Whisk together egg and milk in a small bowl.
5. Mix bread crumbs, flour and Italian seasoning in a medium-sized bowl.
6. Dip zucchini slices in egg wash, then in bread crumb mixture. Fry in olive oil until coating is browned and toasty on both sides.
7. Layer cooked zucchini slices in a small casserole.
8. Top the bottom layer with torn basil, then add the rest of the slices.
9. Top zucchini layers with mozzarella cheese followed by sauce.
10. Top sauce with grated Parmesan cheese.
11. Serve with pasta is desired.

Zucchini Risotto

- 2 tablespoons butter
- 1 small onion, finely diced
- 4 cloves garlic, minced
- ¼ cup white wine
- 1 ½ cups Arborio rice
- 4 cups chicken stock
- 1 small zucchini, shredded
- 2 tablespoons marinated sun-dried tomatoes, chopped
- ½ cup heavy cream
- ½ teaspoon salt
- ¼ teaspoon white pepper
- 2 teaspoons fresh thyme leaves, chopped
- ¼ cup shredded Parmesan cheese

1. Melt butter in a sauté pan and add onion and garlic, cooking until onion is soft and translucent.
2. Deglaze the pan with white wine and cook until most of the liquid has evaporated.
3. Add the rice and toast lightly.
4. Gradually add chicken stock, stirring continuously, adding more liquid as stock evaporates.
5. When rice mixture becomes creamy. Add zucchini, sun-dried tomatoes, cream, salt, pepper and thyme, cooking until the cream has been incorporated.
6. Add cheese just before serving.

Loaded Venison Spaghetti

- **1 pound ground venison**
- **1 jar spaghetti sauce**
- **½ onion, finely chopped**
- **½ green bell pepper, finely chopped**
- **1 cup shredded zucchini**
- **½ cup baby portabella mushrooms, finely chopped**

1. Sauté onions and bell pepper in a little bit of olive oil until slightly tender; add mushrooms.
2. Add ground venison and cook until meat is browned.
3. Add zucchini and cook until slightly tender.
4. Add spaghetti sauce and simmer until vegetables are soft.
5. Serve over pasta with garlic bread on the side.

Creamy Italian Pasta

- 1 small onion, chopped
- 6 cloves garlic, minced
- 1 pound Italian sausage
- 2 zucchini, shredded
- 3 cups heavy cream
- ½ cup shredded Parmesan cheese
- 1 teaspoon salt
- ½ teaspoon pepper
- ½ cup reserved pasta water
- 1 tablespoon basil leaves, torn

1. Cook pasta according to package instructions; set aside, reserving ½ cup pasta cooking water.
2. Coat the base of a Dutch oven with olive oil and sauté onion and garlic until onion is soft and translucent.
3. Add Italian sausage and cook until browned and crumbled.
4. Add shredded zucchini and cook about a minute more.
5. Add cream, pasta water, salt and black pepper.
6. Bring to a simmer, then add Parmesan cheese and toss with pasta.
7. Serve topped with torn basil leaves.

Will-Not-Miss-the-Meat Vegetable Lasagna

- 2 medium zucchini, diced
- 2 medium yellow squash, diced
- 1 yellow onion, diced
- 1 green bell pepper, diced
- 1 cup sliced portabella mushrooms
- 1 cup baby spinach
- 1 15-ounce can Italian seasoned tomato sauce
- 4 cloves garlic
- 1 ½ cups cottage cheese
- 8 ounces cream cheese, softened
- 1 egg
- 1 package no-boil lasagna noodles
- 1 8-ounce package mozzarella cheese

1. Preheat oven to 375 degrees.
2. Steam vegetables until tender.
3. Mix veggies with tomato sauce and garlic, simmer over medium heat until warm.
4. Meanwhile, blend cream cheese, cottage cheese and egg until fluffy.
5. Spread about ¼ cup of sauce over the bottom of a lasagna pan. Cover with a layer of noodles.
6. Spread a third of the cream cheese mixture over noodles; cover with a third of the remaining sauce.
7. Top sauce with slices of mozzarella cheese.
8. Continue layering, finishing with cheese.
9. Bake for 35 to 45 minutes, until cheese is browned and bubbly.

Chicken and Zucchini Linguini

- ½ box linguini
- 1 pound chicken breast, diced
- 2 medium zucchini, diced
- 1 onion, chopped
- 1 green bell pepper, chopped
- 6 cloves garlic, minced
- ½ cup grated Parmesan cheese
- Juice of one lemon
- ½ teaspoon lemon zest
- ¼ teaspoon crushed red pepper red pepper
- Salt and pepper to taste

1. Prepare linguini according to package instructions; set aside.
2. Sauté onions and bell pepper in olive oil until they begin to tenderize. Add chicken, zucchini, garlic and spices and cook until chicken is no longer pink.
3. Toss chicken mixture with linguini and Parmesan cheese.
4. Top with more cheese if desired.

Zucchini-Spinach Quiche

- 1 frozen pie shell, thawed
- Six slices bacon, cooked and crumbled
- 1 medium zucchini, sliced into thin rounds
- 1 cup baby spinach leaves
- 1 cup half and half
- 4 eggs
- 1 cup Swiss cheese, shredded

1. Preheat oven to 450 degrees, prick pie shell with a fork and cover fully with aluminum foil. Bake for about 8 minutes and remove from oven. Reduce oven temperature to 325 degrees.
2. Line pie shell with zucchini, arranging in a circle with slices overlapping slightly. Cover with spinach leaves.
3. Mix half and half, cream and Swiss cheese.
4. Pour over veggies and bake for about 45 minutes, until center is firm and set.

Shrimp Fettuccini

- ½ box fettuccini pasta, prepared as directed
- 1 cup butter
- 2 medium onions, chopped
- 2 stalks celery, chopped
- 1 green bell pepper, chopped
- 1 medium zucchini, shredded
- 1 tablespoon all-purpose flour
- 1 bag jumbo shrimp, peeled and deveined
- 1 cup half and half
- 8 ounces pasteurized process cheese, cut into chunks
- 3 cloves garlic, minced
- 1 tablespoon hot sauce
- ¼ cup grated Parmesan cheese
- Salt and pepper to taste

1. Prepare pasta as directed, set aside.
2. Melt butter over medium heat and sauté onion, celery and green pepper until almost tender. Add zucchini and cook until all vegetables are tender.
3. Add flour and stir until well blended.
4. Add shrimp and simmer for 5 minutes.
5. Add half and half, cheese, garlic and hot sauce.
6. Bring to a simmer, then reduce heat and cook on low for about 5 minutes.
7. Serve over fettuccini, topped with Parmesan cheese.
8. Serve with salad and garlic bread.

Veggie-Stuffed Macaroni & Cheese

- 1 pound elbow macaroni, cooked to package instructions
- 2 tablespoons butter
- 3 cloves garlic, minced
- ½ yellow onion, finely chopped
- 2 tablespoons flour
- 1 ½ cups cups milk
- ½ cup heavy cream
- 2 cups shredded cheddar cheese
- 1 medium zucchini, shredded
- 2 tablespoons bread crumbs
- 2 tablespoons shredded Parmesan cheese

1. Prepare pasta as directed; set aside.
2. Sauté onion and garlic in butter until soft and tender.
3. Add flour and cook about 2 minutes.
4. Add milk and cook over low to medium heat until sauce is thick and bubbly.
5. Add cheese and stir until melted.
6. Mix pasta with shredded zucchini and pour cheese sauce over both, mixing well.
7. Top with bread crumbs and Parmesan cheese.
8. Bake in a 350 degree oven for 35 to 45 minutes, until cheese is bubbly and bread crumbs are brown and toasted.

Cheesy Beef & Veggie Macaroni Casserole

- 2 cups ground beef, turkey or venison
- ½ yellow onion
- 1 tablespoon butter
- 2 cups cooked pasta
- 2 cups California blend frozen vegetables, thawed
- 1 medium zucchini, shredded
- ¼ cup sour cream
- 1 tablespoon butter
- 1 tablespoon flour
- ¾ cup milk
- ¾ cup shredded sharp Cheddar Cheese
- 4 ounces processed American cheese, cubed
- 1 tablespoon shredded Asiago cheese
- Salt and pepper to taste

1. Preheat oven to 375 degrees.
2. Brown ground meat and onion in a skillet until meat is crumbly and onion is tender.
3. Add shredded zucchini and California blend vegetables and cook until warm.
4. Add cooked pasta, sour cream and butter and cook until butter melts.
5. Meanwhile, melt butter in a small saucepan. Add flour and mix until blended.
6. Add milk and a dash of black pepper and cook, stirring constantly, until thick and bubbly.
7. Slowly add cheese and stir until melted.
8. Pour cheese sauce over meat mixture and pour into a casserole dish.
9. Bake for about 30 minutes, until casserole is warm and bubbly.

Bacon-Infused Chicken & Zucchini over Jasmine Rice

- 2 cups jasmine rice, cooked according to package instructions
- 6 strips bacon
- ½ yellow onion, chopped
- 2 chicken breasts, chopped into small pieces
- 2 heaping tablespoons flour
- 1 ½ cups chicken stock
- 2 medium zucchini, chopped
- 2 cloves garlic
- Dash red pepper flakes
- Salt and pepper to taste

1. Cook rice according to package instructions; set aside.
2. In a medium saucepan, cook bacon until crisp. Pour off excess oil, leaving about 1 tablespoon.
3. Add chopped onion and cook until just beginning to tenderize.
4. Add chicken and cook until no longer pink.
5. Sprinkle chicken with flour and pour in chicken stock, stirring well.
6. Add zucchini, garlic and spices, cooking until sauce is thick and bubbly and zucchini is tender.
7. Serve over jasmine rice.

Sausage & Zucchini with Polenta Cakes

- 1 tube polenta, sliced into ¼-inch rounds
- ¼ cup grated Parmesan cheese
- 1 tablespoon olive oil
- Pinch red pepper flakes
- 1 medium onion, diced
- 3 cloves garlic
- 1 green bell pepper, diced
- 1 pound sweet Italian sausage
- 1 medium zucchini, diced
- 1 cup tomato sauce
- Heat olive oil over medium heat in a sauté pan.
- Add polenta slices and cook until both sides are crispy and browned.
- Transfer to a baking pan and sprinkle with Parmesan cheese; set aside.
- Add additional oil to pan if needed and sauté onion, pepper and garlic until onion is translucent.
- Add Italian sausage and cook until browned.
- Add tomato sauce and zucchini and simmer until zucchini is soft and tender.
- Broil polenta slices until cheese melts.
- Serve sausage and zucchini sauce over polenta cakes.

Serves four.

Fire Roasted Vegetable Pasta

- 9 ounces cherry or grape tomatoes, sliced in half
- 1 large zucchini, diced
- 2 cups Portobello mushrooms, diced
- ¼ cup olive oil
- 3 cloves minced garlic
- 1 tablespoon Italian seasoning
- 1 teaspoon Mediterranean sea salt
- 1/2 teaspoon crushed red pepper
- ½ teaspoon fresh ground black pepper
- Salt to taste
- 2 tablespoons olive oil
- ½ box whole wheat linguini, prepared according to package instructions
- ¼ cup grated Parmesan cheese

1. Preheat oven to 400 degrees.
2. Mix together ¼ cup olive oil, garlic, Italian seasoning, sea salt, crushed red pepper and black pepper. Add tomatoes, zucchini and mushrooms and toss together until well coated.
3. Pour vegetables in a single layer onto a baking pan and roast for 45 minutes to an hour, until soft and caramelized.
4. Meanwhile, cook linguini according to package instructions and set aside.
5. When vegetables are ready, place in a bowl and mash with 2 tablespoons olive oil. Toss together with pasta until well coated, adding Parmesan cheese slowly to incorporate.
6. Serve with additional Parmesan cheese if desired.

Zucchini & Mushroom Tart

- 2 tablespoons butter
- 1 shallot, minced
- 4 cloves garlic, minced
- 3 cups assorted diced mushrooms
- 1 medium zucchini, shredded
- 1 tablespoon fresh thyme leaves
- 2/3 cup heavy cream
- ¼ cup plus one tablespoon freshly grated Parmesan
- 1 egg, beaten
- 16-20 sheet phyllo dough
- 1 teaspoon melted butter

1. Melt butter over medium-low heat and add shallots and garlic. Cook for about 10 minutes, stirring often.
2. Add mushrooms, season generously with salt and fresh ground black pepper and cook until mushrooms have reduced to about half their original size.
3. Add zucchini and thyme leaves and cook about five minutes.
4. Add cream and cheese and remove from heat.
5. Allow mixture to cool slightly, then slowly add beaten egg, stirring quickly to incorporate.
6. Fold phyllo dough sheets in half, and place them in the bottom of a pie pan, alternating tips to cover the base and sides of the pan. Brush with melted butter when all the sheets are in place.
7. Preheat oven to 325 degrees.
8. Pour filling into pie pan and bake for about 45 minutes, until a knife inserted in the tart center comes out clean.

Stuffed Zucchini Rolls

- 1 tablespoon oil
- 1 small onion, chopped
- 2 cloves garlic, minced
- 8 ounces ground turkey
- ½ cup chopped zucchini
- ½ cup chopped mushrooms
- 1 cup chopped spinach
- ½ cup ricotta cheese
- ¼ cup shredded Parmesan cheese
- 2 large zucchini, julienne sliced
- 2 cups marinara sauce
- ½ cup shredded mozzarella cheese
- ¼ cup shredded Parmesan cheese

1. Salt zucchini slices and place in a colander for excess water to drain.
2. Heat olive oil in a large sauté pan and add onion and garlic, cooking until tender and translucent.
3. Add ground turkey and cook until browned.
4. Add chopped zucchini and chopped mushrooms, cooking until both are tender.
5. Add spinach, ricotta and ¼ cup Parmesan cheese; set mixture aside to cool.
6. Pat zucchini slices dry.
7. When mixture is cool enough to handle, spoon about a tablespoon onto the end of each zucchini slices, rolling it up snuggly and placing it in a casserole dish.
8. Repeat until zucchini slices are gone.
9. If you have any remaining stuffing, sprinkle it over the top of the zucchini rolls, then cover all with the marinara sauce.
10. Sprinkle cheeses on the top.
11. Bake in a 375 degree oven for about 35 minutes, until cheeses are toasty and melted.

Manicotti with Zucchini & Italian Sausage

- 8 manicotti, cooked to package instructions
- 1 tablespoon olive oil
- ½ yellow onion, finely diced
- 2 cloves garlic
- 8 ounces Italian sausage
- 1 medium zucchini, shredded
- 2 tablespoons cream cheese
- 2/3 cup ricotta cheese
- ½ cup plus ¼ cup mozzarella cheese
- ½ cup Parmesan cheese, divided
- 2 cups tomato sauce

1. Cook manicotti and set aside.
2. Line a sauté pan with olive oil and add onion and garlic, cooking over medium heat until onion is soft and translucent. Add Italian sausage and cook until browned and crumbled.
3. Add zucchini and cook about three minutes more.
4. Remove from heat and add cream cheese, stirring until melted.
5. Allow mixture to cool, then add ricotta, ½ cup mozzarella and ¼ cup Parmesan cheeses, stir to mix well.
6. Spoon ½ cup sauce over the bottom of a 9/13-inch casserole dish.
7. Spoon filling into manicotti shells and place them in the casserole.
8. Pour the remaining sauce over the top of the stuffed manicotti and top with remaining ¼ cup mozzarella and ¼ cup Parmesan cheese.
9. Bake in a 375 degree oven for 30 minutes, until heated through.

Curried Chicken & Veggies

- 1 onion, diced
- 3 or 4 chicken breasts, cut into pieces
- Pinch of salt and black pepper
- 1 pound baby carrots, cut in half lengthwise
- 6 cups chicken stock
- 3 tablespoons curry powder
- 1 tablespoon garam masala
- 2 small zucchini, diced
- 1 small yellow squash, diced
- 1 tablespoon butter

1. 4 servings instant couscous, prepared as per package instructions with 1 teaspoon garam masala added to cooking water.
2. Coat a Dutch oven with olive oil and add onion and chicken. Season with salt and pepper and cook until chicken is no longer pink.
3. Add carrots, chicken stock, curry powder and garam masala. Simmer, covered, about 15 minutes.
4. Add zucchini and yellow squash and simmer about 15 minutes more, until carrots are tender.
5. Stir in butter.
6. Serve in bowls over couscous and plenty of the sauce.

Zucchini, Basil & Bacon Pizza

- 1 pizza crust, unbaked
- 1 8-ounce can Italian-seasoned tomato sauce
- 1 cup mozzarella cheese, shredded
- 1 medium zucchini, thinly sliced
- 6 slices bacon, cooked and crumbled
- ¼ cup basil leaves, sliced in a chiffonade
- Sea salt and freshly ground pepper

1. Spread tomato sauce over pizza crust.
2. Top with cheese, sliced zucchini, crumbled bacon and basil.
3. Season with salt and pepper to taste.
4. Bake in a 400 degree oven until cheese is bubbly, about 20 minutes.

DESSERTS

Zucchini gives sweet treats a hint
of moisture that is sure to be a hit, while
allowing you to hide veggies in the
tastiest of ways.

Zucchini Citrus Cake

- 2 ½ cups flour
- 2 ½ teaspoons baking powder
- ½ teaspoon salt
- ¾ cup butter, softened
- 2 cups sugar
- 3 eggs
- 1 cup zucchini, grated
- 1 ¼ cup milk
- 2 teaspoons lemon juice
- 2 teaspoons lime juice
- 1 teaspoon vanilla
- 1 teaspoon lemon zest
- 1 teaspoon lime zest
- powdered sugar

1. Preheat oven to 375 degrees.
2. Blend flour, baking powder and salt, set aside.
3. Cream butter and sugar together until fluffy.
4. Add eggs, one at a time, beating well after each addition.
5. Add vanilla, lemon juice and lime juice and beat well.
6. Mix zucchini, milk and citrus zest together.
7. Alternately add flour mixture and zucchini mixture to batter, mixing between additions, until ingredients are well blended.
8. Pour into a greased and floured 9x13 inch baking pan.
9. Bake for 30 to 40 minutes, until cake is golden brown and a toothpick inserted near the center comes out clean.
10. After cake has cooled, sprinkle with powdered sugar.

Banana Pudding Cake

- **2 ripe bananas, mashed**
- **½ cup shredded zucchini**
- **1 ¼ cup milk**
- **¾ cup butter, softened**
- **1 ¾ cups sugar**
- **3 eggs**
- **1 ½ teaspoons vanilla**
- **2 ½ cups flour**
- **2 ½ teaspoons baking powder**
- **½ teaspoon salt**
- **1 box instant vanilla pudding mix**

1. Preheat oven to 350 degrees.
2. Blend bananas, zucchini and milk; set aside.
3. Mix flour, baking soda, salt and pudding mix; set aside.
4. In a medium bowl, cream butter until light and fluffy. Gradually add sugar and mix well. Add eggs, one at a time, and blend well.
5. Alternately add flour mixture and banana mixture, mixing between additions, until ingredients are well blended.
6. Pour into a greased Bundt pan and bake for 50 to 55 minutes or until cake tests done.
7. Drizzle with Sugar Glaze.

SUGAR GLAZE: Mix two cups confectioners' sugar with two tablespoons milk and a dash of vanilla. Stir until smooth. Drizzle over Banana Pudding Cake.

Chocolate Zucchini Sheet Cake

- **2 cups flour**
- **2 cups sugar**
- **1/2 cup butter, softened**
- **½ cup chocolate chips**
- **½ cup vegetable oil**
- **¼ cup baking cocoa**
- **1 cup shredded zucchini**
- **½ cup milk**
- **½ teaspoon baking soda**
- **2 eggs**
- **1 teaspoon vanilla extract**

1. Preheat oven to 350 degrees.
2. In a mixing bowl, combine flour and sugar/
3. In a medium saucepan over medium heat, bring butter, chocolate chips, vegetable oil and cocoa to a boil.
4. Pour chocolate mixture over flour and sugar; blend well.
5. In a small bowl, mix zucchini, milk and baking soda. Add to cake mixture and blend well.
6. Lightly beat eggs with vanilla and add to cake mixture, mixing until just blended.
7. Bake for 30 to 40 minutes, until a toothpick inserted into the center comes out clean.

FROSTING: Melt ½ cup butter, ½ cup chocolate chips, 3 tablespoons heavy cream and 1 cup powder sugar over medium heat, stirring constantly. Whisk until smooth and spread over hot cake.

Zucchini-Pineapple Pound Cake

- 1/2 cup shortening
- 1 cup butter, softened
- 2 ¼ cups sugar
- 6 eggs
- 3 cups flour
- 1 teaspoon baking powder
- ¼ cup buttermilk
- 1 teaspoon vanilla extract
- ½ cup crushed pineapple with liquid
- 1 cup shredded zucchini
- 1 recipe Pineapple Topping

1. In a medium bowl, cream together shortening, butter and sugar.
2. Add eggs, one at a time, blending well between each addition.
3. Mix flour and baking soda; set aside.
4. Blend milk and vanilla extract; set aside.
5. Alternately add flour mixture and milk mixture to batter, mixing well.
6. Add pineapple and zucchini and mix until well blended.
7. Pour into a greased and floured Bundt pan.
8. Place in a cool oven; set temperature to 325 degrees.
9. Bake for 75 minutes.
10. After cake is cool, invert from pan and drizzle with Pineapple Topping.

Pineapple Topping: Mix ¼ cup melted butter with 1 cup crushed pineapple and 1 ½ cups confectioner's sugar.

Zucchini Spice Cake

- 2 cups flour
- 1 teaspoon baking powder
- 1 teaspoon baking soda
- 1 teaspoon cinnamon
- ½ teaspoon nutmeg
- ¼ teaspoon allspice
- 3 eggs
- 2 cups sugar
- ½ cup vegetable oil
- ½ cup milk
- ¼ cup sour cream
- 1 teaspoon vanilla

1. Preheat oven to 350 degrees.
2. Combine flour, baking powder, baking soda, cinnamon, nutmeg and allspice.
3. In a separate mixing bowl, beat eggs until light and frothy. Add sugar gradually, beating until blended. Add oil; mix well.
4. Blend zucchini with milk and sour cream.
5. Into egg mixture, blend flour mixture and zucchini alternately, mixing well after each addition.
6. Fold in vanilla, stirring well.
7. Pour into a greased 9x13-inch baking pan and bake in preheated oven for 45 to 50 minutes, until done.
8. When cake is cool, sprinkle with confectioners' sugar.

Walnut Sour Cream Pound Cake

- 2 cups white sugar
- ¾ cup brown sugar
- 1 cup butter, softened
- ½ cup finely shredded zucchini
- ½ cup buttermilk
- 5 eggs
- 3 cups flour
- ½ cup toasted walnuts, finely ground
- ½ teaspoon baking soda
- ½ teaspoon salt
- 1 cup sour cream
- 2 teaspoons vanilla

1. Preheat oven to 350 degrees.
2. Spread ¾ cup walnuts on baking sheet and toast for 5 to 10 minutes; set aside to cool.
3. Cream together sugars and butter until light and fluffy.
4. Add eggs, one at a time, mixing well between additions.
5. Add zucchini and buttermilk and mix well.
6. Mix flour, baking soda and salt together in a separate dish.
7. Finely grind walnuts and add to flour mixture.
8. Alternately add flour mixture and sour cream to sugar mixture, beating well between additions.
9. Stir in vanilla.
10. Pour into a greased and floured 9x13 inch pan and bake for about 45 minutes, until a toothpick inserted into the center comes out clean.
11. Dust with powdered sugar when cool.

Clementine Zucchini Cake

- ½ cup shortening
- 1 cup sugar
- 2 eggs
- ½ cup finely grated zucchini
- 3 teaspoons clementine juice
- 1 teaspoon grated clementine zest
- 1 teaspoon lemon zest
- 2 cups flour
- 2 teaspoons poppy seeds
- ½ teaspoon salt
- ½ teaspoon baking soda
- 2/3 cup buttermilk
- 1 teaspoon vanilla
- ½ cup sugar
- **Juice of two clementines**

1. Preheat oven to 325 degrees.
2. Cream together shortening and sugar until fluffy.
3. Add eggs, one at a time beating well between additions.
4. Add zucchini, zest and clementine juice, mixing well.
5. Mix together flour, poppy seeds, salt and baking soda.
6. Alternately add flour mixture and buttermilk to sugar mixture, beating well between additions.
7. Stir in vanilla.
8. Pour into a greased and floured fluted pan and bake about an hour, or until a toothpick inserted near the center comes out clean.
9. Mix clementine juice and sugar and pour over hot cake.
10. After cake has cooled, remove from pan.
11. Preheat oven to 350 degrees.

Triple Chocolate Zucchini Brownies

- ¾ cup flour
- ¼ teaspoon baking soda
- 3 tablespoons cocoa
- 2 eggs
- 1 cup sugar
- ½ cup butter
- 2 ounces bittersweet chocolate
- ½ cup semi-sweet chocolate chips
- 1 cup shredded zucchini

1. Preheat oven to 350 degrees.
2. Combine flour, baking soda and cocoa; set aside.
3. Beat two eggs in a mixing bowl, add sugar and mix until well blended.
4. Melt chocolates and butter together in a small saucepan over low heat until melted. Add to egg mixture and mix well.
5. Slowly add flour mixture, mixing well after each addition.
6. Stir in zucchini.
7. Pour into a greased 9x13 inch baking pan and bake at 350 degrees for 30 minutes or until a toothpick inserted into the center of the pan comes out clean.
8. Let cool 30 minutes before cutting.

Zucchini Cookies

- 1/2 cup butter, softened
- 1 cup sugar
- 1 egg
- 1 cup grated zucchini
- 2 cups all-purpose flour
- 1 teaspoon baking soda
- 1/2 teaspoon salt
- 1 cup chocolate chips

1. Preheat oven to 375 degrees.
2. In a medium bowl, cream together butter and sugar.
3. Add the egg and beat with mixer until well blended, then stir in the zucchini.
4. Blend the dry ingredients then add to zucchini mixture.
5. Grease cookie sheets, then drop dough by the teaspoonful onto the prepared sheets.
6. Bake in preheated oven for 8 to 10 minutes, allowing cookies to cool slightly on the cookie sheet before removing them to a towel or wire rack to cool completely.
7. Makes about three dozen cookies.

Zucchini Cowboy Cookies

- 1/2 cup butter, softened
- 1 cup sugar
- 1 cup brown sugar
- 2 eggs
- 1 cup grated zucchini
- 1 cup oatmeal
- 2 cups all-purpose flour
- 1 teaspoon baking soda
- 1/2 teaspoon salt
- 1 cup chocolate chips

1. Preheat oven to 375 degrees.
2. In a medium bowl, cream together butter and sugar. Add the egg and beat with mixer until well blended, then stir in the zucchini.
3. Blend the dry ingredients then add to zucchini mixture.
4. Grease cookie sheets, then drop dough by the teaspoonful onto the prepared sheets.
5. Bake in preheated oven for 8 to 10 minutes, allowing cookies to cool slightly on the cookie sheet before removing them to a towel or wire rack to cool completely.

Zucchini Date Bars

- 1 1/2 cups flour
- 1 cup white sugar
- ½ cup brown sugar
- ½ teaspoon baking powder
- ¼ teaspoon salt
- 1 cup vegetable oil
- 4 eggs
- 2 teaspoons vanilla
- 1 ¼ cup chopped dates
- 1 medium zucchini, shredded

1. Preheat oven to 350 degrees.
2. Combine flour, sugars, baking powder, salt, vegetable oil, eggs, vanilla and dates in order listed in mixing bowl, blend well.
3. Pour into a greased 9x13 inch baking pan.
4. Bake at 350 degrees or until top is lightly browned.
5. Cool and cut into bars.

Rustic Zucchini Tart

- 1 ready-to-bake deep dish pie crust
- 3 cups finely diced zucchini, peeled and seeded
- ½ cup sugar
- 2 teaspoons vanilla
- 1 teaspoon cinnamon
- ¼ teaspoon nutmeg
- 2 ½ tablespoons butter, cut into small pieces
- 1 egg
- 2 tablespoons sugar

1. Preheat oven to 400 degrees.
2. Toss zucchini with 1/2 cup sugar, vanilla, cinnamon, nutmeg and butter.
3. Pour into center of pie crust and fold edges over, leaving center of the tart open.
4. Brush with egg wash made from one beaten egg mixed with a splash of water.
5. Dust with sugar.
6. Bake tart for 12 minutes at 400 degrees, then reduce heat to 350 degrees and bake for another 30 minutes, until center filling is caramelized and bubbly.

Watermelon-Zucchini Sorbet

- 1 medium zucchini, peeled and seeded
- 2 cups watermelon, chopped
- ½ cup superfine sugar
- 3 tablespoons corn syrup
- 1 tablespoon lemon juice
- 2 cups vanilla yogurt

1. Blend zucchini, watermelon, sugar, corn syrup and lemon juice until smooth, about two or three minutes.
2. Add yogurt and blend until smooth.
3. Pour mixture into stainless steel container and place in freezer.
4. Stir once an hour until sorbet is set.

27286983R00063

Made in the USA
Middletown, DE
14 December 2015